QUOTES FOR LEADERS

A WEEKLY JOURNAL OF QUOTES TO SPARK VISION, COURAGE, AND EXTRAORDINARY RESULTS

THE QUOTIVATION SERIES

DR. JO LUKINS

ISBN: 978-1-7635127-7-1 (Paperback)

Elite Edge Publishing

www.drjolukins.com

QUOTES FOR LEADERS INVITES YOU TO EXPLORE WISDOM FROM those who have achieved in business, politics, sports, the military, and as thought leaders; carefully selected to support your journey. Set aside time each week to reflect on the quote and consider what it means for you. A diary entry or reminder can help you stay committed.

This journal offers space for your weekly reflections. As you consider each quote, notice which ones resonate and which ones you might question. Both reactions help you better understand your values and approach to performance.

The second part of the book provides further reflection questions. These are designed to give you space for your own thoughts before considering additional prompts.

LOOKING FOR SOME EXTRA ACCOUNTABILITY TO KEEP YOU INSPIRED THROUGHOUT THE YEAR?

YOU CAN CHOOSE TO RECEIVE A WEEKLY EMAIL WITH EACH QUOTE AND THE JOURNAL PROMPTS TO HELP YOU STAY MOTIVATED AND ON TRACK. IF YOU'D LIKE TO RECEIVE A WEEKLY REMINDER, SIMPLY SCAN THE QR CODE BELOW AND YOU'LL START GETTING AN EMAIL WITH THE LATEST QUOTE TO HELP YOU MOVE CLOSER TO YOUR GOALS.

The quotes are organised into five key areas of high performance leadership. If you have a particular area you'd like to focus on, use the guide below to find relevant quotes.

Vision and Purpose:
Quotes 1, 7, 9, 10, 25, 27, 32, 35, 36, 41

Courage and Resilience:
Quotes 4, 12, 13, 24, 27, 32, 33, 37, 40, 44, 49, 52

Integrity and Character:
Quotes 6, 14, 16, 17, 28, 30, 34, 39, 45

Teamwork and Collaboration:
Quotes 3, 5, 15, 22, 23, 28, 31, 38

Example and Action:
Quotes 2, 8, 11, 18, 19, 20, 21, 26, 42, 43, 46, 47, 48, 50, 51

Reflect and Perform

Each page offers a quote to spark reflection about your mindset, routines, and leadership journey. Take your time, revisit the quote over a week, and observe how your views might change with ongoing experience.

Some quotes may be familiar, but their true value comes from thoughtful reflection. Consider how you might apply their message to make a lasting difference in your journey.

Performance-Driven Prompts

- After reflecting, what actions or habits could you apply this week in your leadership?
- If a quote feels at odds with your experience, notice what you believe instead, and let that insight guide you.

In the final section, you'll find space to add quotes you discover throughout the year, allowing your motivation to grow with you.

I look forward to sharing this journey. Reach out to let me know which quotes inspire you, and the impact they have on your performance and mindset. Shine bright, Dr. Jo (excel@drjolukins.com)

Custom copies for your business, team or organization
If you'd like your own set of books from the Quotivation Series, please contact us about creating a custom edition.

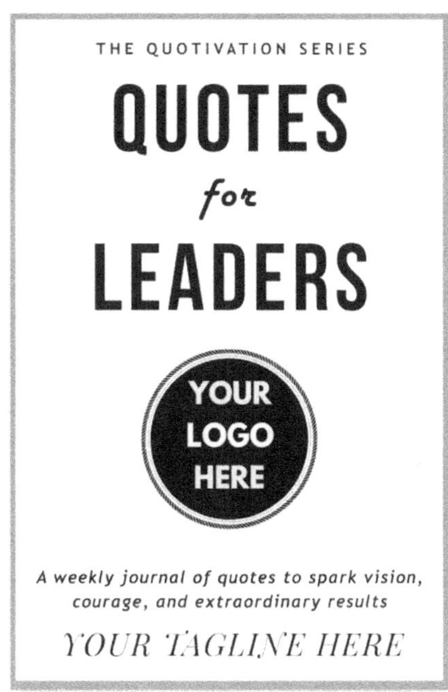

> # A leader is one who knows the way, goes the way, and shows the way.

JOHN C. MAXWELL

WORLD-RENOWNED LEADERSHIP EXPERT AND AUTHOR, MAXWELL GUIDES LEADERS THROUGH PRACTICAL WISDOM AND ACTIONABLE PRINCIPLES

TWO

> I don't go by the rulebook. I lead by the heart, not by the head.

PRINCESS DIANA

PRINCESS DIANA LED WITH COMPASSION, BREAKING ROYAL TRADITION THROUGH EMPATHETIC, CHARISMATIC, AND AUTHENTIC SERVANT LEADERSHIP.

THREE

> Trust is the glue of life. It's the most essential ingredient in effective communication.

STEPHEN COVEY

LEADERSHIP EXPERT COVEY FOSTERED TRUST AND COLLABORATION, VITAL QUALITIES FOR SUCCESSFUL TEAMS AND LEADERS

If you're going through hell, keep going.

WINSTON CHURCHILL

ICONIC BRITISH PRIME MINISTER, CHURCHILL
ENCOURAGED PERSISTENCE AND UNWAVERING
RESOLVE DURING CRISIS AND ADVERSITY

> # If you want to lift yourself up, lift up someone else.

BOOKER T. WASHINGTON

EDUCATION PIONEER, WASHINGTON ADVOCATED SERVICE
AND SUPPORT AS VITAL LEADERSHIP CHARACTERISTICS

Integrity is doing the right thing, even when no one is watching.

C. S. LEWIS

BELOVED AUTHOR-PHILOSOPHER, LEWIS MADE
MORALITY AND UNSEEN VIRTUE CENTRAL
TO LASTING LEADERSHIP LEGACY

Do not go where the path may lead, go instead where there is no path and leave a trail.

RALPH WALDO EMERSON

INFLUENTIAL ESSAYIST, EMERSON CHAMPIONS
COURAGE, ORIGINALITY, AND TRAILBLAZING AS
CORNERSTONES OF LASTING LEADERSHIP

EIGHT

> # Leadership is not position or title, it is action and example.

UNKNOWN

UNIVERSAL PRINCIPLE, REMINDING THAT TRUE
LEADERS SHOW THEMSELVES THROUGH WORK,
NOT RANKS OR STATUS

NINE

> Fortune favors the prepared mind.

LOUIS PASTEUR

GROUNDBREAKING SCIENTIST, PASTEUR
DEMONSTRATED HOW DILIGENCE AND READINESS
FOSTER SUCCESS AND OPPORTUNITY FOR LEADERS

Half of getting what you want is knowing what you have to give up to get it.

BILL PHILLIPS

WELLNESS LEADER, PHILLIPS VALUES SACRIFICE
AND DEDICATION AS KEYS TO EFFECTIVE
GOAL-SETTING AND LEADERSHIP

We are what we repeatedly do. Excellence, therefore, is not an act but a habit.

ARISTOTLE

ARISTOTLE'S ENDURING WISDOM: EXCELLENCE AND VIRTUE GROW FROM CONSISTENT HABITS CENTRAL TO STRONG LEADERSHIP

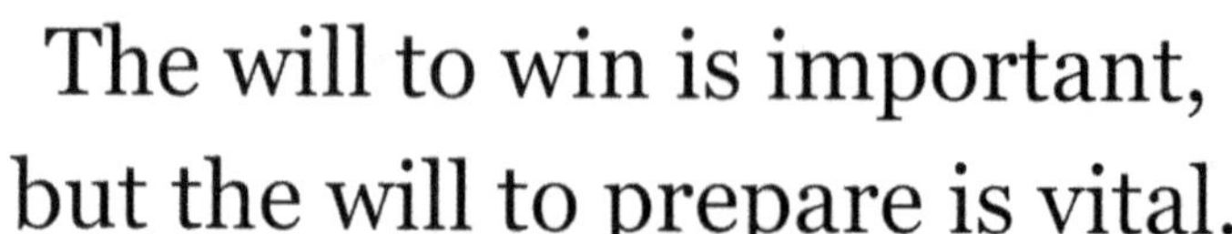

The will to win is important, but the will to prepare is vital.

JOE PATERNO

LEGENDARY COACH, PATERNO PRIORITIZED
PREPARATION AS THE FOUNDATION
FOR COMPETITIVE, EFFECTIVE LEADERSHIP

> Behold the turtle. Who only makes progress when sticking its neck out.

JAMES B. CONANT

DISTINGUISHED SCIENTIST AND EDUCATOR, CONANT
HIGHLIGHTS RISK-TAKING AND BOLDNESS
AS KEYS TO PROGRESS AND LEADERSHIP

FOURTEEN

> Ability will get you to the top, character will keep you there.

JOHN WOODEN

LEGENDARY BASKETBALL COACH, WOODEN ROOTED
LEADERSHIP SUCCESS IN CHARACTER, INTEGRITY, AND
COACHING WISDOM

> # Alone we can do so little; together we can do so much.

HELEN KELLER

INSPIRATIONAL AUTHOR, KELLER'S LEGACY
SPOTLIGHTS COLLABORATION AND INCLUSION
AS KEYS TO MEANINGFUL LEADERSHIP

Discipline is the bridge between goals and accomplishment.

JIM ROHN

LEGENDARY BUSINESS PHILOSOPHER, ROHN
MOTIVATES DISCIPLINE AND PERSEVERANCE
AS CRITICAL TOOLS FOR LEADERSHIP SUCCESS

In matters of principle, stand like a rock.

THOMAS JEFFERSON

FOUNDING FATHER, JEFFERSON PROMOTED
STEADFASTNESS AND MORAL COURAGE AT
THE HEART OF BOLD LEADERSHIP

> # Excellence is not a skill.
> ## It is an attitude.

RALPH MARSTON

INSPIRATIONAL WRITER, MARSTON MOTIVATES
ATTITUDE-DRIVEN EXCELLENCE AS A HALLMARK
OF LASTING LEADERSHIP ACHIEVEMENT

> # Do what you can, where you are, with what you have.

TEDDY ROOSEVELT

U.S. PRESIDENT AND EXPLORER, ROOSEVELT
ENCOURAGED RESOURCEFULNESS AND ACTION
UNDER CHALLENGE TO INSPIRE LEADERS EVERYWHERE

Attention to detail is everything.

MIKE WALDO

WALDO'S COACHING EMPHASIZES THAT CAREFUL,
PRECISE EXECUTION ELEVATES ANY
LEADER'S ACTIONS AND RESULTS

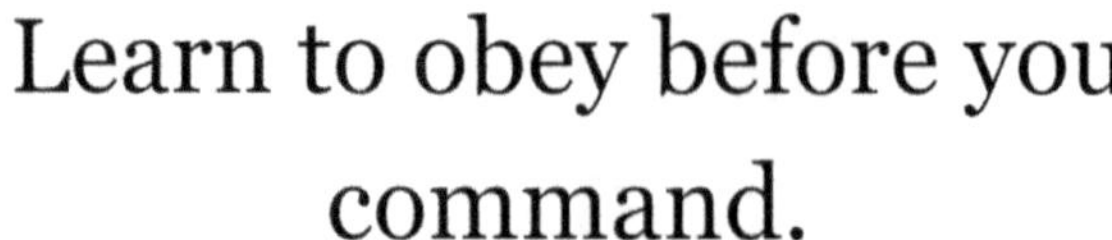

Learn to obey before you command.

GREEK PROVERB

ANCIENT WISDOM TEACHING THE VALUE OF LEARNING
AND HUMILITY FOR FUTURE LEADERS

TWENTY-TWO

> Build your own dreams, or someone else will hire you to build theirs.

FARRAH GRAY

ENTREPRENEUR AND PHILANTHROPIST,
GRAY INSPIRES SELF-DRIVEN GROWTH AND
ENTREPRENEURSHIP IN LEADERSHIP JOURNEYS

TWENTY-THREE

> The strength of the team is each individual member. The strength of each member is the team.

PHIL JACKSON

NBA COACH, JACKSON CHAMPIONED UNITY AND COLLECTIVE SUCCESS, TRANSFORMING TEAMS INTO HIGH-PERFORMING LEADERS

True courage is not the absence of fear, but the willingness to proceed in spite of it.

UNKNOWN

TIMELESS INSIGHT, REMINDING THAT AUTHENTIC
COURAGE IN LEADERSHIP MEANS ACTING
BOLDLY DESPITE INEVITABLE FEARS

> Great leaders are almost always great simplifiers, who can cut through argument, debate and doubt to offer a solution everybody can understand.

GEN. COLIN POWELL
MILITARY LEADER, POWELL MODELED CLARITY
AND DECISIVE ACTION TO RESOLVE
CHALLENGES IN LEADERSHIP DYNAMICS

> Before you are a leader, success is all about growing yourself. When you become a leader, success is all about growing others.

JACK WELCH

CEO, WELCH FOSTERED PEOPLE-FOCUSED LEADERSHIP, ENCOURAGING LEADERS TO NURTURE AND DEVELOP OTHERS' GREATNESS

> # All battles are won before they are fought.

SUN TZU

ANCIENT STRATEGY MASTER, SUN TZU TAUGHT
FORESIGHT, STRATEGY, AND PLANNING
AS VITAL LEADERSHIP SKILLS

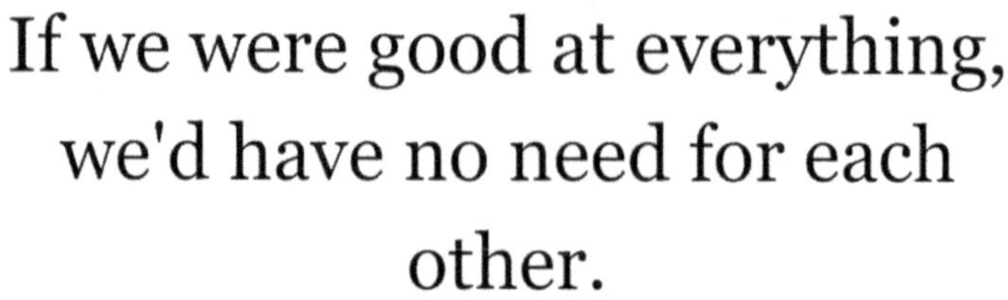

> If we were good at everything, we'd have no need for each other.

SIMON SINEK

RENOWNED THINKER, SINEK CHAMPIONS TEAMWORK FOR ORGANIZATIONAL LEADERSHIP AND INNOVATION

No one can make you feel inferior without your consent.

ELEANOR ROOSEVELT

HUMANITARIAN LEADER WHO CHAMPIONED DIGNITY, JUSTICE, AND HUMAN RIGHTS AS GUIDING PRINCIPLES FOR GLOBAL CITIZENSHIP; US FIRST LADY 1933-1945

> # Our lives begin to end the day we become silent about things that matter.

MARTIN LUTHER KING, JR.

CIVIL RIGHTS ICON, KING MODELED SPEAKING OUT FOR JUSTICE AS EVERY LEADER'S RESPONSIBILITY AND GIFT

> # If you command wisely, you'll be obeyed cheerfully.

THOMAS FULLER

HISTORICAL WRITER, FULLER VALUED WISE LEADERSHIP
AND HARMONY AS FACTORS FOR STRONG TEAMS' SUCCESS

Success is that place in the road where preparation meets opportunity.

BRANCH RICKEY

HALL-OF-FAME BASEBALL EXECUTIVE, RICKEY EMBRACED
READINESS AND CHARACTER IN LEADERSHIP
BREAKTHROUGH MOMENTS

THIRTY-THREE

> Hard work beats talent when talent doesn't work hard.

TIM NOTKE

BASKETBALL COACH, NOTKE DELIVERS A POWERFUL MESSAGE ON DILIGENT EFFORT AS ESSENTIAL FOR LEADERSHIP EXCELLENCE

> ## If you have integrity, nothing else matters. If you don't have integrity, nothing else matters.

ALAN SIMPSON

FORMER U.S. SENATOR, SIMPSON UNDERSCORED
INTEGRITY AS THE PILLAR OF TRUSTWORTHY AND
EFFECTIVE LEADERSHIP

> # Vision without action is a daydream. Action without vision is a nightmare.

JAPANESE PROVERB

UNIVERSAL WISDOM, CONNECTING PURPOSEFUL
VISION WITH PRACTICAL ACTION REQUIRED
FOR EFFECTIVE LEADERSHIP SUCCESS

> # The best way to predict your future is to create it.

PETER DRUCKER

PIONEERING MANAGEMENT THEORIST, DRUCKER
EMPHASIZED PROACTIVE LEADERSHIP IN SHAPING
ORGANIZATIONAL SUCCESS AND INNOVATION

> # We may encounter many defeats, but we must not be defeated.

MAYA ANGELOU

ESTEEMED POET AND ACTIVIST, ANGELOU CELEBRATED
RESILIENCE AND HOPE AS A LEADER'S STRENGTH IN
OVERCOMING CHALLENGES

Nothing great was ever achieved without enthusiasm.

HENRY DAVID THOREAU

INFLUENTIAL THINKER, THOREAU EMPHASIZED
PASSION AND ENERGY AS CRUCIAL FOR INSPIRING
AUTHENTIC LEADERSHIP

> If you look at what you have in life, you'll always have more. If you look at what you don't have in life, you'll never have enough.

OPRAH WINFREY

MEDIA ICON, WINFREY ADVOCATES GRATITUDE
AND ABUNDANT MINDSET FOUNDATIONAL FOR
MEANINGFUL LEADERSHIP AND GROWTH

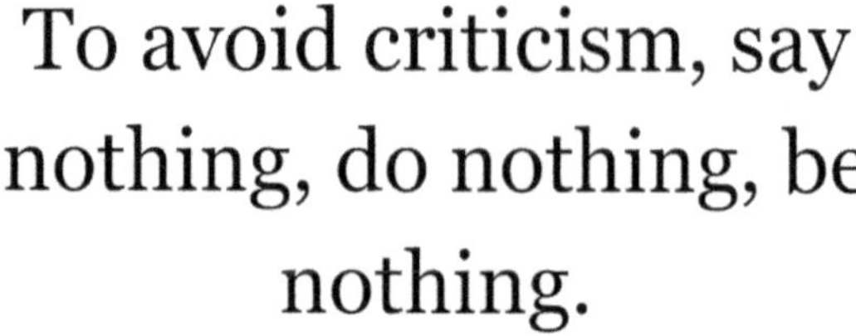

To avoid criticism, say nothing, do nothing, be nothing.

ARISTOTLE

ARISTOTLE HIGHLIGHTED COURAGE AND
AUTHENTICITY, WARNING LEADERS AGAINST
PASSIVITY IN PURSUIT OF IMPACT

Great minds have purposes, little minds have wishes.

WASHINGTON IRVING

ESTEEMED AMERICAN AUTHOR, IRVING STRESSES
PURPOSEFUL INTENTION OVER IDLE
WISHING AS A LEADERSHIP HALLMARK

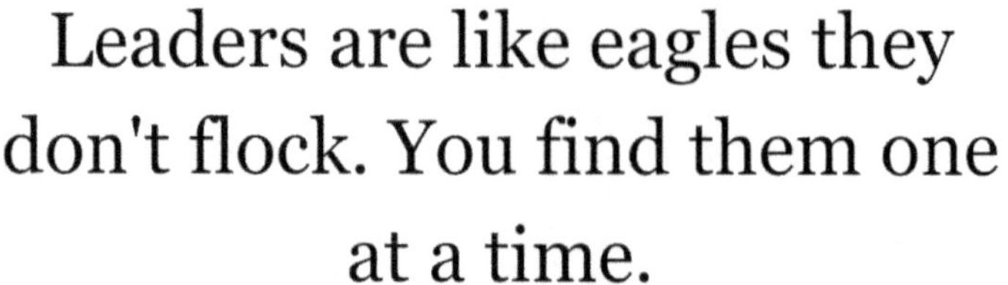

Leaders are like eagles they don't flock. You find them one at a time.

KNUTE ROCKNE

FAMED COACH, ROCKNE PROMOTED
INDIVIDUALITY AND RARE LEADERSHIP
QUALITIES IN EVERY EXCEPTIONAL LEADER

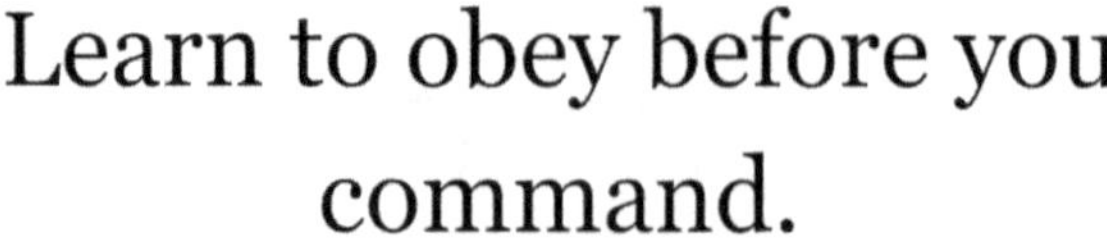

Learn to obey before you command.

GREEK PROVERB

ANCIENT WISDOM TEACHING THE VALUE OF
LEARNING AND HUMILITY FOR FUTURE LEADERS

"

Nothing can stop the man with the right mental attitude from achieving his goal nothing on earth can help the man with the wrong mental attitude.

THOMAS JEFFERSON

JEFFERSON'S LEADERSHIP LEGACY RESTS ON POSITIVE
MINDSET AND DETERMINATION ABOVE CIRCUMSTANCE

> # To be successful, you don't have to do extraordinary things. Just do ordinary things extraordinarily well.

JOHN ROHN

BUSINESS PHILOSOPHER, ROHN INSPIRED LEADERS
TO DELIVER EXCELLENCE THROUGH EVERYDAY
ACTS AND CONSISTENT PERFORMANCE

Leadership is practiced not so much in words as in attitude and in actions.

HAROLD S. GENEEN

CEO AND BUSINESS INNOVATOR, GENEEN
UNDERSCORED CONSISTENT ACTIONS OVER
EMPTY RHETORIC FOR IMPACTFUL LEADERSHIP

Before you are a leader, success is all about growing yourself. When you become a leader, success is all about growing others.

JACK WELCH

CEO, WELCH FOSTERED PEOPLE-FOCUSED
LEADERSHIP, ENCOURAGING LEADERS TO
NURTURE AND DEVELOP OTHERS' GREATNESS

Discipline is the bridge between goals and accomplishment.

JIM ROHN

LEGENDARY BUSINESS PHILOSOPHER, ROHN
MOTIVATES DISCIPLINE AND PERSEVERANCE
AS CRITICAL TOOLS FOR LEADERSHIP SUCCESS

> # When the whole world is silent, even one voice becomes powerful.

MALALA YOUSAFZAI

EDUCATION ACTIVIST WHO CHAMPIONS COURAGE, EQUALITY, AND GIRLS' EDUCATION AS FUNDAMENTAL HUMAN RIGHTS

> # I refuse to believe you can not be empathic and strong.

DAME JACINDA ADERN

FORMER NEW ZEALAND PRIME MINISTER, MODELS
EMPATHETIC LEADERSHIP FOR VALUES-DRIVEN
GOVERNANCE .

> # Leaders and learning are indispensable to each other.

JOHN F. KENNEDY

PRESIDENT KENNEDY ADVOCATED LIFELONG LEARNING
AS A NON-NEGOTIABLE FOR EVERY EFFECTIVE LEADER

The only easy day was yesterday.

U.S. NAVY SEALS

ELITE MILITARY ETHOS, SEALS INSTILL RESILIENCE
AND CONTINUAL EFFORT IN LEADERSHIP
UNDER DEMANDING CIRCUMSTANCES

 You'll find my reflection questions in the following section. They've been included separately so you can first explore your own ideas and see what stands out to you.

As a leader, this is your chance to stretch your thinking, challenge your habits, and connect each concept to your training and performance in a real and personal way.

Once you've completed your initial reflections, take a moment to read through the additional questions. See what sparks your curiosity or pushes you to think differently. Go back to your earlier notes and build on them; this is where real growth happens.

This process is designed to help you get the most from your reflections and keep your focus on progress, not perfection. Your effort in this space will be reflected in how you show up in your leadership and your life.

DR. JO

ONE

 A leader is one who knows the way, goes the way, and shows the way.

JOHN C. MAXWELL

Leadership demands both vision and consistent action, inspiring trust as a role model. True leaders guide others by walking the path themselves. Their success is grounded in clarity, trust, and visible example.

- How do you demonstrate the path forward to your team?
- Are you inspiring others by your actions and decisions?
- What steps make your leadership visible and supportive?

TWO

 I don't go by the rulebook, I lead by the heart, not by the head.

PRINCESS DIANA

Leadership that prioritizes empathy, compassion, and authenticity inspires connection and trust, creating meaningful relationships and positive change.

- How do you let empathy guide your leadership?
- What actions show your team you lead with heart, not just authority?
- How can you balance intuition and logic in your leadership approach?

 Trust is the glue of life. It's the most essential
ingredient in effective communication.

STEPHEN COVEY

Trust forms the bedrock of strong relationships and collaboration. Leaders who cultivate trust enable honest and open communication. With trust, teams achieve greater cohesion and success.

- How do you model trustworthiness and integrity?
- What can you do to build trust among your team?
- How do your communications promote transparency and mutual respect?

FOUR

 If you're going through hell, keep going.

WINSTON CHURCHILL

Persistence through adversity forges resilient leaders. Progress is achieved by refusing to give up in tough times. Lead others by encouraging courage and hope against challenge.

- How do you encourage persistence during tough times?
- What strategies help you to keep moving forward in adversity?
- How will you support your team when challenges seem overwhelming?

FIVE

 If you want to lift yourself up, lift up someone else.

BOOKER T. WASHINGTON

Growth as a leader comes from raising others up. Serving and empowering teammates strengthens organizational culture. Selfless leaders support, motivate, and create pathways for others.

- Who can you support in achieving their potential today?
- What opportunities exist to empower someone else on your team?
- How will you measure the impact of helping others?

SIX

 Integrity is doing the right thing, even when no one is watching.

C. S. LEWIS

Leadership anchored in integrity inspires trust and confidence. Ethical decisions, even in private, establish lasting respect. Leaders set standards through quiet acts of honesty and principle.

- Are you making decisions based on values, not convenience?
- How do you maintain ethical standards in unseen moments?
- What example does your integrity set for future leaders?

SEVEN

> Do not go where the path may lead, go instead where there is no path and leave a trail.

RALPH WALDO EMERSON

Innovation and originality are vital to lasting leadership. Trailblazers enable others to follow new directions with confidence. Legacy is built by the courage to explore and create.

- What innovative ideas are you willing to pursue this week?
- How are you modeling courage and originality?
- What legacy will your actions create for your team?

EIGHT

> Leadership is not position or title, it is action and example.

UNKNOWN

Leaders earn respect through their choices and behaviors, not authority. Influence grows from initiative and service. Anyone can lead by consistently making positive choices for others.

- How do your actions demonstrate your leadership values?
- What example do you set for others?
- How can you empower others to lead by example?

NINE

> Fortune favors the prepared mind.

LOUIS PASTEUR

Preparation turns opportunity into achievement in leadership. Ready leaders respond effectively to unexpected challenges and good fortune. Investments in learning and readiness set teams apart.

- What steps are you taking to increase preparedness?
- How do you encourage your team to anticipate opportunities?
- Are you nurturing a culture of readiness?

TEN

> Half of getting what you want is knowing what you have to give up to get it.

BILL PHILLIPS

Leaders make progress by understanding and accepting necessary sacrifices. Effective goal setting requires thoughtful evaluation of trade-offs. Strategic choices lead teams to sustained achievement.

- What are you willing to sacrifice for team success?
- How will you evaluate necessary trade-offs in upcoming decisions?
- Are you leading discussions on goal setting and prioritization?

ELEVEN

> We are what we repeatedly do. Excellence, therefore, is not an act but a habit.

ARISTOTLE

Success is a result of consistent habits and daily discipline. Leaders set standards by modeling patterns of excellence. Teams thrive when routine actions align with ambitious goals.

- How are you modeling habits of excellence?
- What repeated behaviors make your team successful?
- How can you help others develop productive habits?

TWELVE

> The will to win is important, but the will to prepare is vital.

JOE PATERNO

Preparation underpins ambition and leads to sustainable achievement. Leaders prioritize readiness over mere desire. Practice and planning create confident teams.

- What are you doing to ensure thorough team preparation?
- How do you prioritize preparation over mere ambition?
- What support is needed to enhance readiness within your organization?

THIRTEEN

 Behold the turtle. Who only makes progress when sticking its neck out.

JAMES B. CONANT

Risk-taking and boldness are required for leadership growth. Advancing as a leader means embracing uncertainty and stepping outside comfort zones. Courage is the driver of progress.

- What risks are you willing to take as a leader right now?
- How do you encourage others to step outside their comfort zones?
- How will you measure progress by courageous actions?

FOURTEEN

 Ability will get you to the top, character will keep you there.

JOHN WOODEN

Talent opens doors, but lasting success depends on character. Leaders earn enduring influence by prioritizing integrity. Humility and ethical conduct shape organizational culture.

- How do you prioritize character development?
- What values define your leadership journey and decisions?
- How will your character inspire others during difficulty?

FIFTEEN

Alone we can do so little; together we can do so much.

HELEN KELLER

Collaboration and teamwork magnify a leader's impact. Diverse strengths blend to forge extraordinary achievements. Leaders foster shared goals, unity, and celebration of collective success.

- How are you promoting teamwork and inclusion?
- What new collaborations can you pursue for greater outcomes?
- How do you celebrate shared victories with others?

SIXTEEN

Discipline is the bridge between goals and accomplishment.

JIM ROHN

Discipline provides structure to translate vision into reality. Persistent effort and self-control support long-term achievement. Leaders empower progress with standards of accountability.

- How do you practice discipline in your daily habits?
- What systems support accountability and follow-through in your team?
- How will you help others maintain discipline in pursuing goals?

SEVENTEEN

In matters of principle, stand like a rock.

THOMAS JEFFERSON

Principled leadership emerges from clarity and courage in values. Standing firm in ethical standards provides direction and confidence. Leaders inspire others by unwavering commitment to beliefs.

- How do you uphold core principles during challenging situations?
- What values will you defend regardless of external pressure?
- Are you setting a standard for principled leadership within your organization?

EIGHTEEN

Excellence is not a skill. It is an attitude.

RALPH MARSTON

Mindset determines the level of excellence leaders pursue. Attitude-driven motivation ignites higher performance. Leaders inspire growth and optimism through belief in possibility.

- How do you foster an attitude of excellence in your team?
- What belief systems drive your pursuit of improvement?
- Are you projecting optimism and enthusiasm as a leader?

NINETEEN

Do what you can, where you are, with what you have.

TEDDY ROOSEVELT

Resourcefulness and adaptability are vital qualities for impactful leadership. Leaders make the best use of what's available. Initiative and practical problem-solving drive meaningful change.

- How are you making the best use of available resources?
- What small steps can you take toward leadership goals today?
- How can you empower others to act resourcefully now?

TWENTY

Attention to detail is everything.

MIKE WALDO

Careful execution elevates leadership results and credibility. Leaders distinguish themselves through focus and follow-through. Small details compound into big achievements and trust.

- How do you encourage attention to detail within your team?
- What systems insure precision and quality in your leadership tasks?
- Are you reinforcing the importance of follow-through and careful planning?

TWENTY-ONE

Learn to obey before you command.

GREEK PROVERB

The best leaders develop humility and understanding before taking charge. Serving and listening cultivate empathy and insight. Experience and learning create effective, respected authority.

- What have you learned from the leadership of others?
- How do you value humility and listening in your role?
- Are you encouraging learning and servant leadership in your team?

TWENTY-TWO

Build your own dreams, or someone else will hire you to build theirs.

FARRAH GRAY

Leaders take ownership of their vision and drive purposeful action. Pursuing meaningful goals fuels engagement and satisfaction. Those who lead with independence become innovators and motivators.

- Are you building your own vision or serving someone else's goal?
- How do you inspire others to pursue their dreams?
- What steps can you take towards independence and impact?

TWENTY-THREE

> The strength of the team is each individual member. The strength of each member is the team.

PHIL JACKSON

Unity and empowerment create unstoppable teams. Mutual reliance amplifies impact and fosters belonging. Leaders multiply success by supporting both team and individual strengths.

- How are you investing in every member of your team?
- Do you recognize and nurture individual strengths for team success?
- What fosters unity and belonging in your team?

TWENTY-FOUR

> True courage is not the absence of fear, but the willingness to proceed in spite of it.

UNKNOWN

Bravery is shown by acting even when afraid. Courageous leaders move forward through uncertainty and risk. Action despite fear creates momentum and growth for all.

- How do you encourage action during uncertainty?
- What helps you move forward when feeling afraid?
- Are you celebrating courageous actions in yourself and your teammates?

TWENTY-FIVE

> Great leaders are almost always great simplifiers, who can cut through argument, debate and doubt to offer a solution everybody can understand.
>
> GEN. COLIN POWELL

Leaders succeed by delivering clarity in complexity. Clear thinking and communication simplify challenges and create momentum.

- How do you clarify challenges and solutions?
- How do you simplify your messages?
- What actions help cut through confusion and indecision?

TWENTY-SIX

> Before you are a leader, success is all about growing yourself. When you become a leader, success is all about growing others.
>
> JACK WELCH

Progress shifts from self-development to helping others develop. Servant leaders nurture greatness and invest in their teams. Growth multiplies when leaders make others' potential their priority.

- How do you focus on growing your team, not just yourself?
- Are you mentoring others for development and success?
- What does servant leadership look like for you this week?

TWENTY-SEVEN

 All battles are won before they are fought.

SUN TZU

Preparation and strategy determine successful outcomes. Leaders plan carefully and anticipate obstacles before taking action. Victory is the result of thoughtful, proactive effort.

- How do you prepare your team for upcoming challenges?
- How do you look for obstacles before taking action?
- What planning practices ensure readiness and success?

TWENTY-EIGHT

 If we were good at everything, we'd have no need for each other.

SIMON SINEK

Interdependence makes teams and leaders stronger. Recognizing strengths and weaknesses promotes collaboration and innovation. Delegation and teamwork unlock everyone's contribution.

- How do you leverage others' strengths and fill your own gaps?
- Are you encouraging diversity and collaboration in your team?
- How does relying on others shape your leadership?

TWENTY-NINE

 No one can make you feel inferior, without your consent.

ELEANOR ROOSEVELT

Confident leaders know others' opinions only define them if they accept them, so they refuse belittling messages and protect their self-worth while modelling healthy boundaries.

- Where are you letting others' criticism shape your view?
- When someone makes you feel small, how can you respond in a way that stays grounded in your own values and strengths rather than in their approval?

THIRTY

 Our lives begin to end the day we become silent about things that matter.

MARTIN LUTHER KING, JR.

Leadership means speaking up for justice, even when it is difficult. Leaders build legacy by defending values and taking a stand. Silence undermines mission, while advocacy inspires change.

- How do you use your leadership voice for important causes?
- Are you defending values that matter in tough moments?
- What issues require your advocacy and leadership today?

THIRTY-ONE

 If you command wisely, you'll be obeyed cheerfully.

THOMAS FULLER

Effective leadership earns cooperation by treating people with respect and wisdom. Wise leaders foster goodwill and teamwork. Authority founded on empathy inspires enthusiastic support.

- Are you showing wisdom and empathy in giving instructions?
- How do you encourage positive responses to decisions?
- What lessons help you lead with consideration and clarity?

THIRTY-TWO

 Success is that place in the road where preparation meets opportunity.

BRANCH RICKEY

Success happens at the intersection of readiness and good timing. Proactive effort and vision are critical for achievement.

- What preparations will open new doors for you?
- Are you connecting effort with smart opportunities for success?
- How do you nurture a culture of proactive action and readiness?

THIRTY-THREE

Hard work beats talent when talent doesn't work hard.

TIM NOTKE

Effort matters more than natural ability in the long run. Diligent leaders persist beyond obstacles and inspire others to give their best. Results follow those who outwork and outlast every challenge.

- How do you role model effort and determination?
- What motivates you to overcome obstacles with effort?
- How do you encourage persistence over natural talent?

THIRTY-FOUR

If you have integrity, nothing else matters. If you don't have integrity, nothing else matters.

ALAN SIMPSON

Integrity is the foundation of trustworthy and effective leadership. Without integrity, achievement and influence quickly unravel. Leaders must protect their reputation by acting with honesty and virtue.

- How are you prioritizing integrity in leadership decisions?
- Do your actions inspire trust and confidence?
- What steps safeguard your integrity across all circumstances?

THIRTY-FIVE

> Vision without action is a daydream. Action without vision is a nightmare.

JAPANESE PROVERB

Effective leaders balance planning and purposeful action. Vision gives direction, while action brings results. Both are needed for successful leadership and team outcomes.

- How do you link vision with action?
- Are you planning carefully to achieve meaningful results?
- What actions execute your vision without chaos or distraction?

THIRTY-SIX

> The best way to predict your future is to create it.

PETER DRUCKER

Proactive leadership shapes results and future direction. Leaders act on ideas instead of waiting for opportunity. Intentional effort turns possibilities into reality.

- How will you create the future you want for your team?
- What steps ensure proactive leadership and goal setting?
- Are you encouraging initiative and accountability in shaping outcomes?

THIRTY-SEVEN

 We may encounter many defeats, but we must not be defeated.

MAYA ANGELOU

Resilience and hope are vital qualities in meaningful leadership. Leaders overcome setbacks by sustaining belief and perseverance. Never surrender momentum, even in challenge or loss.

- Are you showing resilience when things don't go as planned?
- How do you help your team overcome setbacks?
- What practices encourage optimism and persistence in hard times?

THIRTY-EIGHT

 Nothing great was ever achieved without enthusiasm.

HENRY DAVID THOREAU

Energy and passion drive successful leaders. Enthusiasm inspires others to join, contribute, and excel. The leader's spirit is contagious and sparks lasting achievement.

- How do you model passion and enthusiasm?
- What energizes you to overcome setbacks?
- Are you encouraging excitement and optimism among your team?

THIRTY-NINE

> If you look at what you have in life, you'll always have more. If you look at what you don't have in life, you'll never have enough.

OPRAH WINFREY

Gratitude cultivates abundance and satisfaction for leaders and teams. Focusing on strengths and resources fuels motivation and possibility. Leaders who model appreciation inspire others to flourish.

- How do you lead with gratitude in daily actions?
- What strengths and resources will you celebrate this week?
- Are you reinforcing abundance mindset for your team?

FORTY

> To avoid criticism, say nothing, do nothing, be nothing.

ARISTOTLE

Courage and authenticity are hallmarks of impactful leaders. Being willing to face scrutiny and take action creates progress. Leaders succeed by engaging with challenges instead of staying passive.

- How will you grow from feedback?
- Are you leading by example even when risking critique?
- What helps you push past fear of judgment to make a difference?

FORTY-ONE

 Great minds have purposes, little minds have wishes.

WASHINGTON IRVING

Leaders achieve more by setting purposeful intentions and acting decisively. Wishing is passive, while purpose moves teams forward. Meaningful impact stems from clear goals and committed effort.

- How do you make purpose central to your decisions?
- Are you inspiring purposeful plans?
- What actions can you take today toward purposeful leadership?

FORTY-TWO

 Leaders are like eagles they don't flock. You find them one at a time.

KNUTE ROCKNE

Exceptional leadership is rare, distinguished by individuality and courage. The strongest leaders act with independence and example. Uniqueness in vision and action sets leaders apart.

- How do you embrace individuality within your leadership role?
- What makes your approach distinctive and impactful?
- Are you seeking unique perspectives to improve your team?

FORTY-THREE

Learn to obey before you command.

GREEK PROVERB

Humility and learning make leaders more effective when directing others. Leadership grows from understanding teammates' perspectives, because serving first builds empathy and legitimacy.

- How have you practiced humility during authority?
- Do you listen and learn before giving direction?
- Are you mentoring new leaders in the value of learning before leading?

FORTY-FOUR

Nothing can stop the man with the right mental attitude from achieving his goal nothing on earth can help the man with the wrong mental attitude.

THOMAS JEFFERSON

A leader's success depends more on mindset than circumstances or talent, so leaders must continually build a positive attitude and resilience in themselves and others.

- How do you encourage positive attitude in your leadership journey?
- How do you reinforce resilience and determination?
- What daily habits keep your mindset on achievement?

FORTY-FIVE

> To be successful, you don't have to do extraordinary things. Just do ordinary things extraordinarily well.

JOHN ROHN

Extraordinary leadership is built from excellence in everyday actions. Committing to high standards in routine tasks delivers success. Leaders inspire by showing that every moment matters.

- How are you modeling excellence in key tasks?
- Do you challenge others to elevate their daily tasks?
- Are you celebrating small wins as steps toward achievement?

FORTY-SIX

> Leadership is practiced not so much in words as in attitude and in actions.

HAROLD S. GENEEN

Influential leaders use attitude and behavior to create impact. Consistent, positive action proves leadership far more than talk. Teams watch what you do more than what you say.

- Are your actions consistent with your messages?
- How do you display the right attitude in challenges?
- Are you coaching others to lead through attitude and example?

FORTY-SEVEN

Before you are a leader, success is all about growing yourself. When you become a leader, success is all about growing others.

JACK WELCH

The leader's role is to nurture development in others. Success is multiplied by making others the focus. Servant leaders empower and inspire greatness in everyone.

- How do you prioritize the growth of you and your team?
- How do you support learning and development as a daily practice?
- What makes you a mentor and advocate for others?

FORTY-EIGHT

Discipline is the bridge between goals and accomplishment.

JIM ROHN

With discipline, vision turns into concrete achievement. Leaders reinforce accountability and persistent effort. Successful teams maintain commitment, direction, and standards over time.

- How do you maintain discipline to achieve your goals?
- Are you creating routines that reinforce accountability?
- What keeps you and your team on track?

FORTY-NINE

 When the whole world is silent, even one voice becomes powerful.

MALALA YOUSAFZAI

Courageous leadership means choosing to speak when it feels easier or safer to stay quiet. One clear voice can break the silence, spark conversation, and give others permission to step forward.

- Where is silence allowing unfair behaviour to continue?
- Whose voices in your team are quiet or overlooked?
- What is one conversation you will start this week?

FIFTY

 I refuse to believe you can not be empathic and strong.

DAME JACINDA ADERN

Effective leaders show they can listen deeply, care about people's experiences, and still make clear, decisive calls when it matters most. Choosing empathy does not dilute authority; rather it builds trust.

- Where do you hold back empathy because you worry it will make you look soft or less decisive?
- How can you show care and clarity in difficult conversations?
- What behaviours would show your team that kindness and strength are expectations, not opposites?

FIFTY-ONE

 Leaders and learning are indispensable to each other.

JOHN F. KENNEDY

Growth and ongoing education define successful leadership. Leaders constantly adapt, evolve, and renew their skills. Teams thrive when leaders make learning central to their role.

- How do you foster continual learning?
- Are you staying current and relevant in leadership knowledge?
- What steps are you taking to encourage growth?

FIFTY-TWO

 The only easy day was yesterday.

U.S. NAVY SEALS

True leadership demands constant resilience and effort. Each day brings fresh challenges and opportunities for growth. Teams overcome adversity by committing to ongoing improvement and endurance.

- What difficult challenge are you stepping up to today?
- How will you inspire resilience and determination?
- Are you reinforcing a culture of perseverance and striving for excellence?

OTHER QUOTES TO INSPIRE

Use this section to collect quotes that inspire you throughout the year. Add a few notes about why each quote stands out or what it means to you personally.

The Quotivation Series is a collection of reflective quote journals designed to take short bites of wisdom, and applying it in a practical way to your upcoming success.

Quotes for Athletes: *A weekly journal of quotes for grit, motivation and a winning mindset.*

Quotes for Coaches: *A weekly journal of quotes for leadership, motivation and excellence.*

Quotes for Referees: *A weekly journal of quotes for focus, poise and resilience.*

Quotes for Business: *A weekly journal of quotes for strategy, growth and success.*

Quotes for Leaders: *A weekly journal of quotes for vision, courage, and inspired achievement.*

Quotes for Investors: *A weekly journal of quotes for patience, clarity and a successful investors mindset.*

Quotes for Stoic Leadership: *A weekly journal of quotes for courage, discipline, and an unbreakable mindset in service.*

Quotes for Parenting: *A weekly journal of quotes for patience, guidance, and love.*

Quotes for Students: *A weekly journal of quotes for focus, persistence and curiosity.*

Quotes for You: *A weekly journal of quotes for growth, self-discovery, and an empowered mindset.*

The Quotivation Series is being released through 2026.
Visit my website **drjolukins.com** to be the first to order your copy or visit your preferred indie bookstore or online platform.

The following books are available at your favourite book store or online platform:

The Elite: Think like an athlete, succeed like a champion. Ten things the elite do differently. 2019

In the Grandstands: The sporting parents guide to raising a confident and happy teen in the highs and lows of youth sports. 2020

The Game Plan: Your 5-month coaching program to champion high performance habits (High Performance Thinking). 2022

The Elite and The Game Plan 2 in 1 Book: Champion your success with elite habits to unleash your winning potential with 10 proven strategies and high-performance coaching program. 2023

Belief: Building unshakeable confidence. 2024

The Whistle Blower: The mental toughness rulebook for referees, umpires, and sports officials. 2025.

The Whistle Blower Workbook: The mental toughness rulebook for referees, umpires, and sports officials. 2025

Referred to as a psychological Indiana Jones, thanks to more than twenty-five years spent exploring what helps people achieve their best. I have enjoyed bringing together these quotes for you. If you'd like to connect or learn more, you can always find me at www.drjolukins.com.

If Quotes for Leaders has made an impact for you, I'd be grateful if you would share your thoughts or leave a review. Similarly, if you'd like to share your favorite quote with me, let me know at excel@drjolukins.com

Shine Bright, Dr. Jo